The Most Beautiful Gusu Fairy Tales

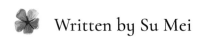 Written by Su Mei

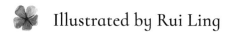 Illustrated by Rui Ling

A Magic Scarf

Books Beyond Boundaries

ROYAL COLLINS

Interpreting Suzhou's Culture through Fairy Tale Picture Books

Wang Quangen

Chinese people are familiar with the saying, "Suzhou and Hangzhou are the heavens on earth."

Suzhou, a beautiful city with a rich culture of 2,500 years, has been an aesthetic inspiration throughout history. Still, depicting Suzhou's culture through illustrated fairy tales was unprecedented. Therefore, Soochow University Press invited Su Mei, a well-known local children's writer, and Rui Ling, an experienced illustrator, to co-create this book series. Aside from its pioneering role in this subject area, it is also the first "cultural picture book" series to combine Chinese elements, regional cultures, ethnic expressions, and fairy tale fantasies. For these reasons, I fell deeply in love with the books' words and images the moment I saw them.

Su Mei has a brilliant imagination and an exquisite style—she is a superb writer. Choosing a topic and putting it into words is a great challenge given Suzhou's colorful and diverse regional culture. Applying the method of time travel in fairy tale writing, Su Mei lets Meiduo'er, an old cat who has been away from Suzhou for a long time, fly back home out of concern for Tiancizhuang, which will soon be pulled down. With the help of a little girl, Nannan, she begins a journey to find her childhood friends ...

Through Meiduo'er's eyes, the author focused on elements that embody the most regional characteristics of Suzhou: river towns, gardens, Taihu Lake, embroidery, ginkgo trees, local snacks, the dialect, and silk. Each element is exemplified in a story; altogether, the stories connect Suzhou's regional cultures and customs effectively. By reading them, children can learn more about Suzhou.

Although the city's beauty is hard to delineate with lines and colors, illustrator Rui Ling did an excellent job in making the works vivid, engaging, and diverse.

I sincerely offer my congratulations on the publication of *The Most Beautiful Gusu Fairy Tales*. I hope that all children can benefit from Suzhou's splendid landscape and glorious culture.

WANG QUANGEN is a professor and doctoral advisor at the School of Chinese Language and Literature of Beijing Normal University, vice president of the Children's Literature Committee of the China Writers Association, and director of the China Children's Literature Education Research Center. He is also vice president of the Asia Children's Literature Research Academy, deputy director of the Professional Committee of Chinese Language Teaching in Chinese Contemporary Literature Research, and review expert of The National Social Science Fund of China. As a distinguished academic, he enjoys a special government allowance for life.

About the Writer:

Su Mei is a member of the China Writers Association and director of the China Society for the Studies of Children's Literature. She now teaches at Soochow University. Su has published over six hundred fairy tales and more than sixty story collections. Her math and science fairy tale picture books have been exported to Singapore, Malaysia, Thailand, Indonesia, and other countries. Many of her works have been selected for Chinese textbooks for kindergartens and US elementary schools. Su is the winner of many awards, including the "Second China Children's Book Gold Award," "Bing Xin Children's Literature Award," "Bing Xin Children's Book Award," and second place in the "First Sina Flash Fairy Tale Competition."

About the Illustrator:

Zhang Ruiling is a professional illustrator and picture book painter. Born in Heze, Shandong Province, Zhang studied at the Department of Design at Shandong College of Art and the Department of Photography at Beijing Film Academy. Her published works include *I Have a Date with Zhuangzi*, etc. Zhang was the winner of the "2012 Bing Xin Children's Book Award."

The weather was getting cold, and people were putting on sweaters and scarves.

Auntie Ding was going back to Beijing soon. "The silk in Suzhou is very famous. I want to buy some silk scarves for my friends."

"Great! I want to buy some, too," said Meiduo'er. "Let's go together."

They came to Guanqian
Street and walked into an
old and famous silk store.

There were so many silk scarves in the store, on the table, on the shelves, and on the walls. It was so hard to choose!

After a long time, they finally decided.

Auntie Ding bought five scarves, and Meiduo'er bought two, one for herself and another for Nannan.

Two days later, Auntie Ding set off for Beijing.

Meiduo'er and Nannan went to visit Grandpa and Grandma Sugar Porridge (an old couple who make sugar porridge).

On their way, a gust of wind blew off Meiduo'er's scarf.

"Mrs. Wind must want to try on your beautiful scarf, too!" laughed Nannan.

"I will share it, but please don't take it away!" cried Meiduo'er.

She didn't have her flying carpet with her, so they ran after the scarf.

A fashion show was taking place in the park, and a model who was about to go on stage could not find her top. Just then, she saw the scarf flying towards her, so she quickly caught it and wrapped it around herself, making it into a beautiful top.

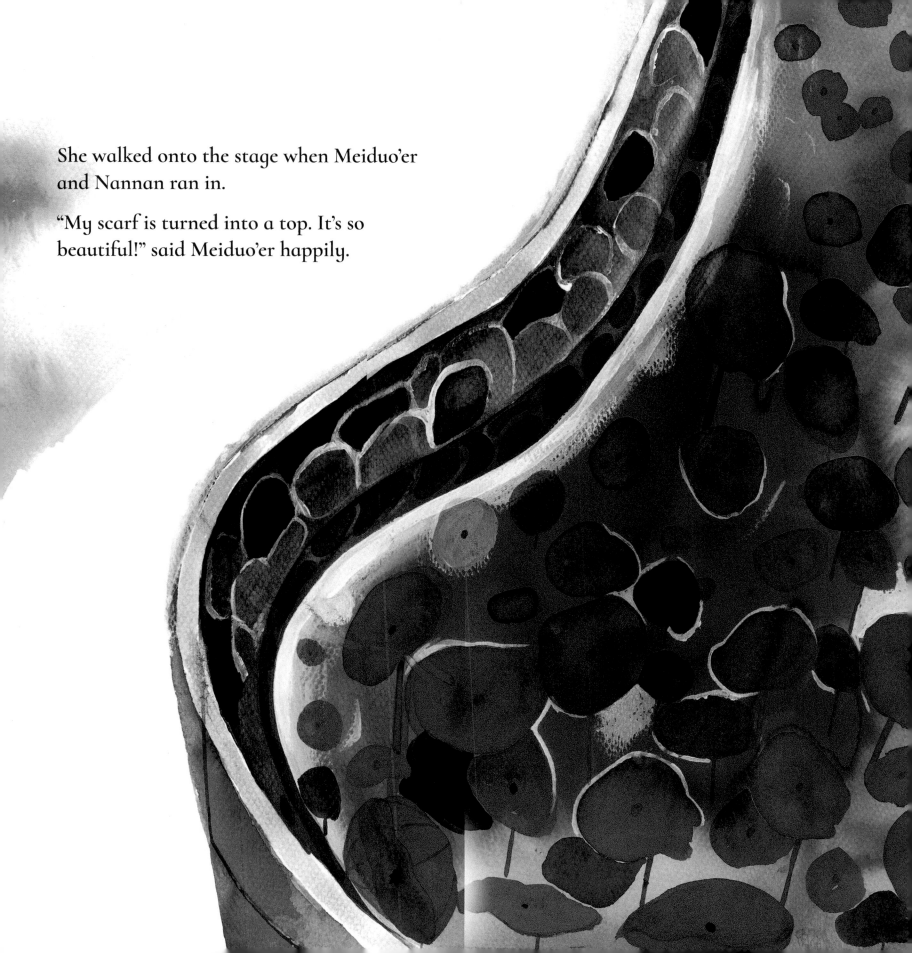

She walked onto the stage when Meiduo'er and Nannan ran in.

"My scarf is turned into a top. It's so beautiful!" said Meiduo'er happily.

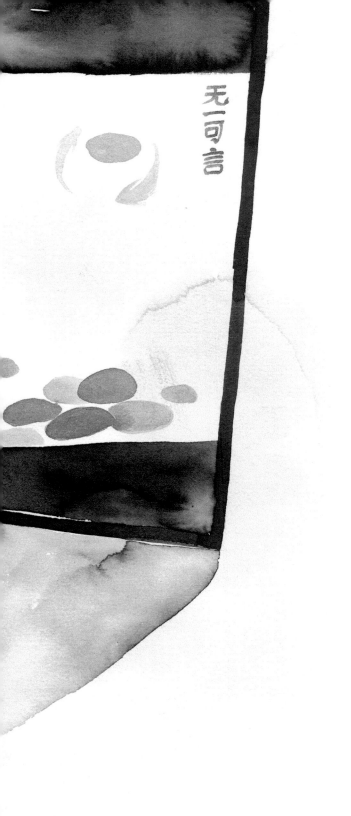

When the show was over, the model returned the scarf to Meiduo'er.

"Thank you for this scarf. Let me help you put it on," she said as she put it around Meiduo'er's neck and made a lovely bow.

The next performance was a magic show. It was Nannan's favorite.

The magician filled the stage with flowers, and the next second, he threw candies and sweets to the audience. Everyone was having great fun!

"Next, please enjoy the rabbit dance! Our bunnies will borrow one special item from one lucky audience to complete their dance. Don't worry. You'll have it back when their dance is over."

The magician waved his wand, and a group of bunnies appeared on stage.

"Hey, they are all wearing my scarf!" Meiduo'er looked down and saw her scarf was not there anymore.

When the dance was over, the magician waved his wand, and the scarf with the bow returned to Meiduo'er's neck again.

Everyone clapped their hands and cheered, "Bravo!"

"Bravo to Meiduo'er's magic scarf!" said Nannan.

Then, Meiduo'er saw San Wangzi in the crowd.

"Hello again," she said.

"My home is nearby. Please come. But I'm the only one home," said the puppy.

They walked into a small, empty room.

"Please sit. I'll bring you some water."

Meiduo'er was shocked when she saw the white silk handkerchief covering the teacup.

"Where did you get this handkerchief?" she asked hurriedly.

"It was my father's most cherished belonging. After he left, I used it to cover the teacups from dust."

"It was mine! I gave it to Awang. I embroidered the winter blossom on it! Is your father Awang?"

"Yes, I'm his son. The Wang in my name is from him," replied San Wangzi.

"Why did you say your father was called Yiquan?"

"My father died saving a child in a fire. People called him Yiquan to commemorate his courage and loyalty."

"I misunderstood. Where's your mother?"

"I never had a mother," said San Wangzi sadly.

Meiduo'er remembered the double-sided embroidery of Awang she had seen, and the picture of him the little boy Jie had cut from the magazine, which probably recorded his heroic deed. She also remembered that in front of Tiger's Tomb, Tiger told her that Awang was like him now, falling into an eternal sleep.

All pieces came together now in Meiduo'er's mind.

"The magic scarf brought me to San Wangzi, and the silk handkerchief helped me find Awang. Silk is my lucky charm!" said Meiduo'er emotionally.

"Are we still going to Grandpa and Grandma Sugar Porridge's place?" asked Nannan.

"Of course! San Wangzi, please come with us. I'll tell Grandpa and Grandma Sugar Porridge about my adventure."

Meiduo'er put her arms around San Wangzi and said, "Sweetie, I'll move in with you tomorrow. I'll always be by your side in the future."

"I will come to visit you every day. Let's be best friends forever!" said Nannan.

Hand in hand, the three friends went to visit Grandpa and Grandma Sugar Porridge.

Knowledge Station

Suzhou, known as the "Silk Capital," is the birthplace of silk. The Taihu Lake region preserves the remains of the Neolithic and Paleolithic eras, bearing witness to the long history of silk.

Mulberry planting, silkworm raising, and production activities of reeling and silk weaving were recorded in the Suzhou region as early as 2,000 years ago.

❀ Silk decoration pendant

❀ Silk weaving machine

Suzhou silk was famous worldwide in the Ming and Qing dynasties. It was listed as one of the three most notable products of southeastern China, together with Nanjing and Hangzhou brocades. Silk of various types is still an important traditional product in Suzhou today, and it is playing a vital role in the history of silk culture in China and the world.

Silkworms eating mulberry leaves

Silk cocoon

The production of silk involves three procedures: reeling, weaving, and dyeing.

Reeling is to extract silk from the cocoon. One cocoon can contain 800–1,000 meters of cocoon silk, consisting of two separate pieces of single silk. Several cocoons of silk will make a piece of raw silk.

Weaving divides raw silk into warp threads and weft threads and interlaces them in a specific pattern to create silk fabric.

Dyeing includes distillation, coloring, printing, and arrangement.

The campus of Suzhou No. 10 High School of Jiangsu Province used to be a part of the Suzhou Weaving Department and an imperial garden in the Qing Dynasty (1616–1912). During their six visits to the Jiangnan region, Emperor Kangxi and Emperor Qianlong both stayed in this garden.

Cao Yin, son of Emperor Kangxi's nanny, was once the young Emperor's learning companion and later served as the Director of the Weaving Department. He was also the grandfather of Cao Xueqin, the author of the groundbreaking masterpiece *Dream of the Red Chamber*. Inside the garden, there is a famous piece of Taihu Stone called Ruiyunfeng that is known for its outstanding exquisiteness.

The old site of the Suzhou Weaving Department

Silk pajamas for women

Suzhou silk products include scarves, qipaos, dresses, shirts, pajamas, handkerchiefs, mini bags, cellphone containers, purses, and slippers.

Nannan's Stories

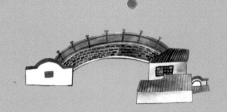

Legend of Silk

Chinese people believe Leizu, the Yellow Emperor's wife, was the first to raise silkworms. She was known as the "Ancestor of Silkworms."

One day, Leizu was drinking in a wild mulberry forest, and some wild silkworm cocoons fell into her bowl. When she picked them out, she noticed the silk kept growing longer and longer. So Leizu began to weave with the silk and then to raise domestic silkworms. Leizu was remembered as the "Ancestor of Silkworms" and was worshipped by empresses of all following dynasties.

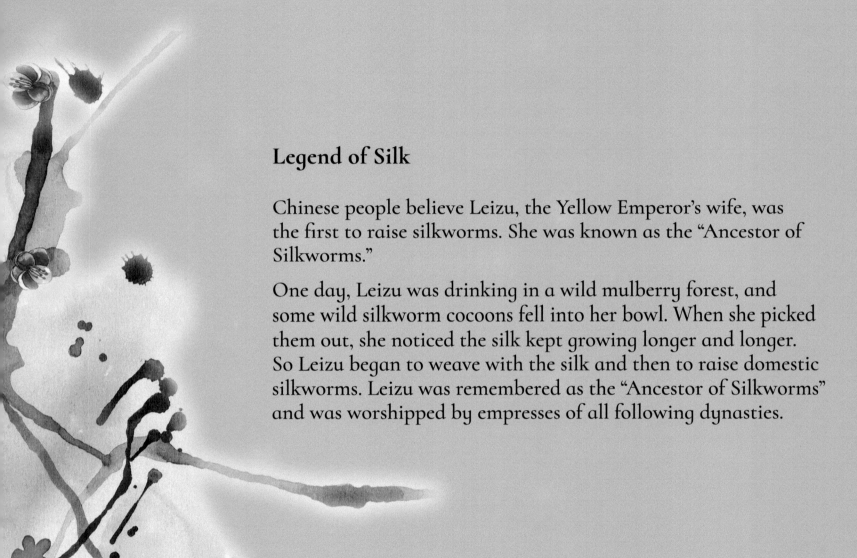

The Ancestor of Silkworms Temple in Shengze, Suzhou City, built in 1827, is the only preserved temple for silk worship.

There is also a Leizu Temple in Xiangfusi Alley in Suzhou. This is where the silk weaving industry worships their patriarch, the Yellow Emperor.

In Suzhou folklore, Leizu is the youngest of the Yellow Emperor's three daughters. It is said that the Yellow Emperor invented the weaving machine with the help of the twelve heavenly beasts and then invented the weaving comb, based on his youngest daughter's comb, to prevent the silk from breaking.

The Most Beautiful Gusu Fairy Tales:
A Magic Scarf

Written by Su Mei
Illustrated by Rui Ling
Translated by Wu Meilian

First published in 2024 by Royal Collins Publishing Group Inc.
Groupe Publication Royal Collins Inc.
BKM Royalcollins Publishers Private Limited

Headquarters: 550-555 boul. René-Lévesque O Montréal (Québec)
H2Z1B1 Canada
India office: 805 Hemkunt House, 8th Floor, Rajendra Place, New
Delhi 110 008

Original Edition @ Soochow University Press

ISBN: 978-1-4878-1187-7

To find out more about our publications,
please visit www.royalcollins.com.